Contents   **3**

Foreword

Canada is a vast and rugged land. From north to south it spans more than half the Northern Hemisphere; from east to west it stretches almost 4,700 miles (7,560 km) across six time zones. It is the second largest country in the world. But it has only one-half of one percent of the world's population. Most of that small population lives in a narrow ribbon of cities stretched out along the U.S. border, leaving huge tracts of untouched territory.

Canada's black-blue lakes, numerous rivers, majestic western mountains, rolling central plains, and forested eastern valleys make it one of the most beautiful countries in the world. The country's beauty is matched by its bounty. Canada has provided fish and furs to Europe since the 1500s. Today, Canada is a world leader in agricultural production, telecommunications, and energy technologies and production. Canada's isolation, unspoiled landscapes, vast distances between cities, and even its extremes of weather have inspired world-renowned painters, such as the Group of Seven and Emily Carr, and famous writers, such as Margaret Atwood, Margaret Laurence, and William O. Mitchell.

Despite all Canada has accomplished, it is a rather young country—and it is still going through growing pains. The French and English fought over Canada after its "discovery" in the late 1400s. The debate continues today between the Province of Quebec and the rest of Canada. In the decades to come, issues such as First Nations governance and the transition from an agricultural to an industrial economy will be part of Canada's development into a mature country. Helping Canada through these growing pains are its long tradition of social democracy and its new-found strength in a diverse multicultural society.

Countries of the World

Canada

Brian Williams

Tom Carter and Ben Cecil, Consultants

NATIONAL GEOGRAPHIC
WASHINGTON, D.C.

Contents

Falkirk Council	
LB	
Askews	
J971	£7.99

This book introduces this vast country, covering its human and physical geography, varied ecosystems, First Nations and newcomer histories, politics, and traditional and modern economic activity. At the start of the last century, Canada's promise lay in its agricultural and industrial force. At the dawn of the 21st century, Canada continues to demonstrate its wealth through its resource industries—but it also shows new promise through advanced industry and high technology as Canada continues to build its young country through the strength of a diverse population.

▲ **Red rowboats at Maligne Lake in the Rocky Mountains are a reminder of human impact, even in Canada's huge wilderness areas.**

Ben P. Cecil, Ph.D.
Head of the Department of Geography
Faculty of Arts, University of Regina

A Vast
and
Rugged
Land

WHEN NEWS BROKE in 1897 that gold had been found in western Canada, a hundred thousand treasure hunters set off for the Yukon. Only a third made it. Many gave up. Others died from the bitter cold or starved. Some survived crossing the mountains only by eating their horses. A railroad replaced Dead Horse Trail through White Pass in 1898, but by then the gold rush was already virtually over.

Getting around can still be difficult in Canada—although not quite so difficult. One reason is its size. It takes almost five days and nights to cross it by train. Only Russia is bigger. Yet Canada is also one of the world's most sparsely settled countries. There are ten Americans for every Canadian.

◀ **Morant's Curve along the Bow River is named after a Canadian Pacific Railway photographer who took some of his most famous shots of trains at this point.**

At a Glance

WHAT'S THE WEATHER LIKE?

Winter winds sweep cold across much of Canada, chilling the air to below freezing and covering the land with thick snow. The western coast of British Columbia is the wettest part of Canada, soaked by over 100 inches (250 cm) of rain a year, mostly in the fall and winter. Summers are generally cool, but it can get hot in southern Canada. The prairies are the driest regions. The map opposite shows the physical features of Canada. Labels on this map and on similar maps throughout this book identify places pictured in each chapter.

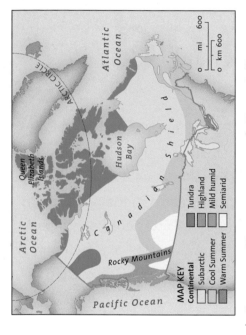

MAP KEY
Continental
Subarctic
Cool Summer
Warm Summer

Tundra
Highland
Mild humid
Semiarid

Average Temperature & Rainfall

Average High/Low Temperatures; Yearly Rainfall

SAINT JOHN (NEW BRUNSWICK):
70° F (21° C); 12° F (-11° C); 44 in (112 cm)

OTTAWA (ONTARIO):
80° F (27° C); 3° F (-16° C); 34 in (87 cm)

MONTREAL (QUEBEC):
79° F (26° C); 5° F (-15° C); 40 in (102 cm)

REGINA (SASKATCHEWAN):
81° F (27° C); -7° F (-22° C); 15 in (38 cm)

VANCOUVER (BRITISH COLUMBIA):
74° F (23° C); 33° F (1° C); 47 in (119 cm)

INUVIK (NORTHWEST TERRITORIES):
56° F (16° C); -18° F (-28° C); 6 in (14 cm)

Fast Facts

OFFICIAL NAME: Canada

FORM OF GOVERNMENT: Federal parliamentary state

CAPITAL: Ottawa

POPULATION: 31,629,000

OFFICIAL LANGUAGES: English, French

MONETARY UNIT: Canadian dollar

AREA: 3,849,674 square miles (9,970,610 sq km)

BORDERING NATION: United States (Greenland is an Overseas Region of Denmark)

HIGHEST POINT: Mount Logan, 19,551 feet (5,959 meters)

LOWEST POINT: Sea level, east, west, and northern coasts

MAJOR MOUNTAIN RANGES: Rockies, Coast, Laurentian Mountains

MAJOR RIVERS: St. Lawrence, Mackenzie, North and South Saskatchewan, Athabasca, Fraser

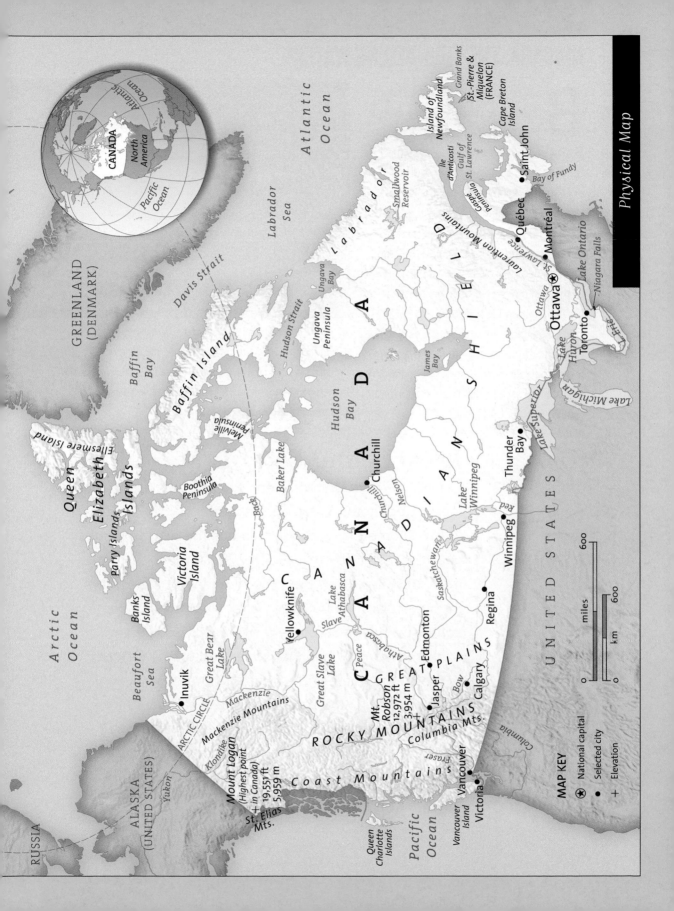

Physical Map

RUSSIA

ALASKA
(UNITED STATES)

Arctic Ocean

GREENLAND
(DENMARK)

Atlantic Ocean

CANADA

North America

Pacific Ocean

Beaufort Sea

Inuvik

Yukon

Klondike

Mackenzie

ARCTIC CIRCLE

Mackenzie Mountains

Mount Logan
(Highest point
in Canada)
19,551 ft
5,959 m

St. Elias
Mts.

Queen
Charlotte
Islands

Coast Mountains

Pacific
Ocean

Vancouver
Island

Victoria

Vancouver

Fraser

Columbia Mts.

Columbia

ROCKY MOUNTAINS

Mt.
Robson
12,972 ft
3,954 m

Jasper

Bow

Calgary

Edmonton

GREAT PLAINS

Regina

Athabasca

Peace

Great Slave
Lake

Lake
Athabasca

Slave

Yellowknife

Great Bear
Lake

Banks
Island

Victoria
Island

Parry Islands

Queen
Elizabeth
Islands

Ellesmere Island

Boothia
Peninsula

Baker Lake

Back

CANADIAN SHIELD

Churchill

Nelson

Churchill

Melville
Peninsula

Baffin Island

Baffin
Bay

Davis Strait

Hudson Strait

Ungava
Peninsula

Ungava
Bay

Hudson
Bay

James
Bay

Lake
Winnipeg

Red

Winnipeg

Saskatchewan

Thunder
Bay

Lake Superior

Lake Michigan

Lake
Huron

Toronto

Lake Ontario

Lake Erie

Niagara Falls

Ottawa

Ottawa

Montréal

St. Lawrence

Québec

Laurentian Mountains

Gaspé
Peninsula

Gulf of
St. Lawrence

Île
d'Anticosti

Island of
Newfoundland

Grand Banks

St.-Pierre &
Miquelon
(FRANCE)

Cape Breton
Island

Saint John

Bay of Fundy

Labrador

Smallwood
Reservoir

*Labrador
Sea*

*Atlantic
Ocean*

UNITED STATES

MAP KEY

✪ National capital

● Selected city

+ Elevation

miles   600

0   600
km

0

NIAGARA: THE THUNDERING WATER

Between Lake Erie and Lake Ontario the Niagara River roars over a rock ledge to create the Niagara Falls. One of nature's most impressive sights, the falls have been a must for tourists ever since French priest-explorer Louis Hennepin was the first European to see them in 1678. Sightseers in raincoats board the *Maid of the Mist* for a thrilling, but wet, boat trip close to the falls to gaze at the wall of water—the name Niagara means "thundering water." Brave—or crazy—people have walked across Niagara Falls on tightropes and plunged over the falls in barrels. Sensation-seekers still sometimes attempt foolhardy acts, even though such stunts are illegal.

▲ A helicopter carries tourists above Horseshoe Falls, the Canadian part of Niagara Falls, while the *Maid of the Mist* cruises in the river below. These falls carry 90 percent of the Niagara River's flow. The rest passes over the smaller American Falls.

Records and Contrasts

Canada and the United States share the world's longest boundary between two nations: 3,987 miles (6,416 kilometers). Canada also has the world's longest coastline—151,489 miles (243,798 kilometers). That is more than five times the circumference of the Earth.

Such a large country as Canada contains dramatic contrasts. Nearly 80 percent of Canadians live and work in dynamic cities that cover less than 1 percent of the country's area. The center of the country is rolling prairies, where trucks or trains can travel for hours across grain fields without passing anything taller than a grain elevator. To the west of the prairies rise the peaks of the Canadian Rockies and the

Mackenzie Mountains, which tower over 12,000 feet (4,500 meters) high.

The Canadian Shield, a hilly region of lakes and swamps, stretches across northern Canada. It has some of the oldest rocks that can be seen anywhere on Earth—up to four billion years old. Its hills and ridges were ancient mountains that have been ground down by glaciers, ice sheets that covered the region during ice ages. Nunavut reaches into far northern Canada. The territory—an area like a state—was established for the native Inuit people.

Lakes, Rivers, and Islands

Canada shares four of the five Great Lakes with the United States: Superior, Huron, Erie, and Ontario. The lakes are important for transportation, as is Canada's

▼ A ship passes by the Thousand Islands, a chain of islands in the St. Lawrence Seaway, at twilight. The seaway was a major engineering feat. When it was completed in 1959 deep-draft ships could travel 2,340 miles (3,766 km) from the Atlantic Ocean to Thunder Bay, Ontario, as well as Duluth, Minnesota, in the United States.

TRAIN ADVENTURE

Canada's most famous train, *The Canadian*, crosses the country from Toronto to Vancouver. The trip takes three days and three nights. It is a great way to see the country's diverse landscapes. The train crosses the Canadian Shield, with its ancient rocks, the rippling grainfields of the prairies, and the forests and rivers of Alberta. It reaches the snow-peaked ranges of Jasper National Park in the Rockies. The final descent takes it to the Pacific coast and the relaxed harbor city of Vancouver.

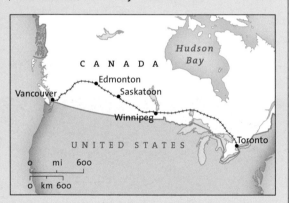

great eastern river, the St. Lawrence. Other rivers in the west and north are less useful for shipping. Some are ice-bound in winter, and some, like the Mackenzie, flow north to the Arctic Ocean, where large container ships cannot travel. Around the coastline are hundreds of islands, including Prince Edward Island in the east and Vancouver Island in the west.

Atlantic Provinces

Eastern Canada was where Europeans made their first settlements. They were pleased to find such fine farming country. The islands and rolling hills get more rain than any other part of Canada except the west coast. The region is good for growing potatoes and raising dairy cattle. Snowfall in winter can be heavy, over 100 inches (250 cm) in New Brunswick and Newfoundland. The fishing villages that dot the coast are a reminder of a centuries-old industry. Fishers traveling to the Grand Banks off Newfoundland were some of the earliest Europeans to reach Canada. So many fish have been caught that there are few left. Today, many people from fishing villages have to make their living from tourism, lumber, or mining.

Quebec

East of Nunavut lies Hudson Bay. This huge inland sea was discovered by Western mariners in 1610, but it was over 200 years before its coast was fully explored. Around the St. Lawrence River in the southeast is fertile farming country, although this is also Canada's prime manufacturing zone.

Quebec is Canada's largest province. Most people here speak French, and the largest city, Montreal, is more French than North American. Quebec City is Canada's oldest city, and its walled Citadel has been declared a World Heritage site. The Citadel is still a base for the Canadian army.

The capital, Ottawa, is home to the government, but it is not Canada's largest city. That title belongs to Toronto, on the north shore of Lake Ontario, a city of

▼ Snow sculptures are lit up at **Ottawa's** famous **Winterlude carnival.**

▲ Saskatchewan farmers haul their grain to an elevator, where it is stored until a train takes it to a mill or a port.

skyscrapers, the Skydome sports stadium, and the soaring CN Tower. Ontario is often described as Canada's "heartland of manufacturing." Its industry has flourished because of nearby supplies of American coal, the province's abundant natural resources, cheap power, and a large labor force.

THE CHINOOK

The Chinook (shi-NOOK) is a "snow-eating" warm wind that blows east from the Rocky Mountains of southwest Canada. As cold air flows down the mountain slopes, it warms up. By the time it reaches low ground, the Chinook is warm enough to melt winter snow. The temperature can rise from freezing to mild in an hour—so fast that skiers may find that the snow is melting beneath their skis!

Prairie Provinces

Before the Canadian Pacific Railroad (CPR) was built in the 1800s, heading west across Canada meant weeks in a riverboat, wagon, or on horseback. The railroad spurred the growth of the prairie provinces—Manitoba, Saskatchewan, and Alberta—which became Canada's "granary." Fields of cereal and other crops seem to stretch to the horizon, and it can be a long drive to school or to have a chat with a neighbor. But there are lively plains cities, too, that reflect the wealth that comes from the region's great reserves of oil, natural gas, and minerals. Edmonton, in Alberta, boasts the world's biggest shopping mall, and Calgary is home to the Calgary Stampede, the world's most famous rodeo show.

Across the Rockies

CPR trains haul passengers and freight across the Rockies, a spectacular ride. Equally breathtaking is

▲ Riders explore Bow Lake, in Banff National Park. The park is Canada's most popular outdoor attraction.

▼ Vancouver's fine natural harbor has made it a prosperous port.

the drive along Alberta's Icefields Parkway, from Lake Louise to Jasper, following the route taken by the early fur trappers. The Rockies are home to numerous national parks that protect the mountain landscape and its wildlife.

British Columbia, with its rugged mountains,

▲ Children play on a frozen lake in the far north of Canada.

▼ Spruce trees line the Mackenzie River for miles.

forests, and dramatic coastline, is much bigger than the U.S. states of California and Oregon combined. The city of Victoria, named after the 19th-century British queen, is often called the most "English" city in North America. Its many tearooms tempt visitors to indulge in an English-style afternoon tea.

WHERE POLAR BEARS LIVE DOWN THE STREET

On the shores of Hudson Bay, beside the Churchill River's mouth, is the "Polar Bear Capital of the World." Polar bears around Churchill have learned that the town's garbage can be an easy source of food without hunting. Churchill can only be reached by rail, air, or sea, but it still attracts many visitors to photograph the bears. Both visitors and residents have to watch out when they pass a dump where a hungry bear may be sniffing out lunch. Some of the bears are so curious that they come right up to tourist buses.

▲ A female polar bear and her cubs wander through the outskirts of Churchill looking for food.

Cold Northlands

Nowhere in Canada is as cold as the far north, in the frozen grip of the Arctic. In Yellowknife, January temperatures never rise above freezing and can drop to –24°F (–32°C). Even the mighty Mackenzie River is ice-covered for nine months of the year. In the winter the sun appears only briefly. The dark sky lights up with the aurora borealis, or northern lights, changing colors caused by particles from the sun colliding with the Earth's atmosphere. Trees find it tough to survive, and farming is not practical. Native Canadians, known as First Nations peoples, live by hunting and fishing. Life is hard work, despite the modern comforts of snowmobiles, television, and the Internet.

Bears and *Beavers*

CANADA'S REMOTE NORTH and extensive forests are home to an exciting range of wildlife, from bears, wolves, beavers, deer, mountain lions, bighorn sheep, and mountain goats to smaller animals such as raccoons, otters, squirrels, and rabbits. The country's lakes and rivers make up about 20 percent of all the fresh water on Earth, and many of them provide excellent fishing. Fishers' favorites include trout, salmon, arctic char, and grayling. Some fishing camps are so remote that they have their own airstrips. But even in remote areas, fishing and hunting are both strictly controlled. Canadians understand the need to protect their wildlife, even in a country where it seems that there is unlimited room for plants and animals to thrive.

◀ In the fall Canada geese migrate south for the winter, traveling as far south as Florida in the United States and even to Mexico.

CONSERVATION IN ACTION

Canada has a proud history of conservation. It has 41 national parks, as well as three marine conservation areas to protect gray whales, sea lions, and other sea life. Canada's first national park was Banff, in Alberta, founded in 1885. Its largest park, which protects herds of bison south of the Great Slave Lake, is five times the size of the United States' Yellowstone National Park. In 1992 Canada became the first industrialized country to ratify the Convention on Biological Diversity—a charter that seeks to protect all of Earth's species.

The Rocky Mountain parks such as Banff, Jasper, and Kootenay offer visitors the chance to catch a glimpse of bears, elk, moose, and bighorn sheep in some of the world's most spectacular scenery.

The map opposite shows vegetation zones—or what grows where—in Canada. Vegetation zones form ecosystems, or environments that support specific plants and animals.

SPECIES AT RISK

Even in a country with as much wilderness as Canada, humans can still threaten plants and animals. The wolf and lynx have been hunted from forests they once roamed, and overfishing has damaged stocks in the Atlantic.

Species at risk include:

>Whooping crane
>Banff snail
>Burrowing owl
>Bison
>White pelican
>Peregrine falcon

>Woodland caribou
>Northern leopard frog
>Swift fox
>Monarch butterfly
>Musk ox
>North Atlantic right whale
>Eastern cougar

▶ Musk oxen huddle together for protection and to keep warm. When wolves attack, adult oxen face outward and use their sharp horns for defense.

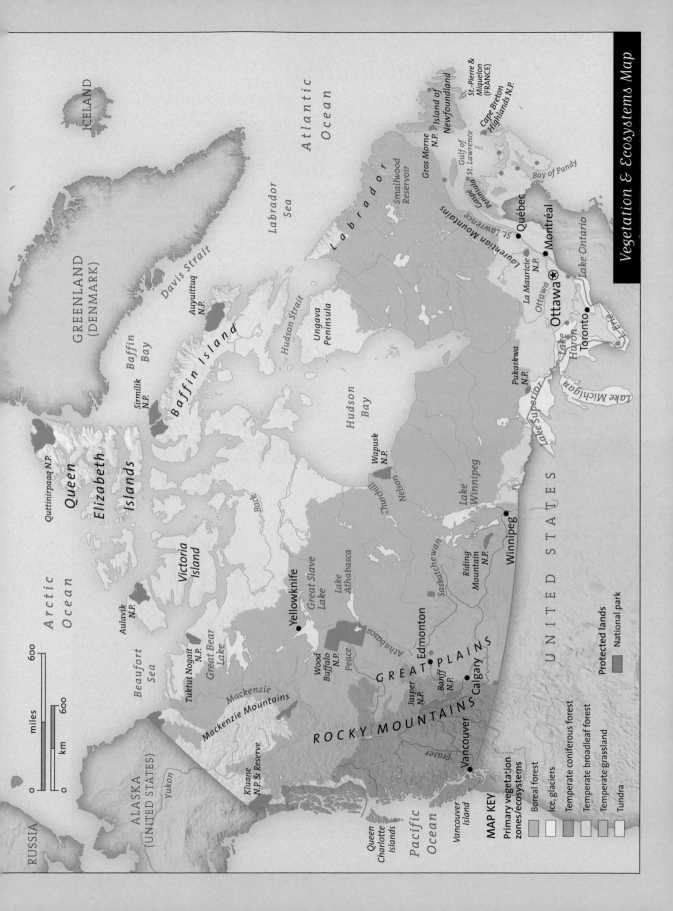

Vegetation & Ecosystems Map

RUSSIA

ICELAND

GREENLAND
(DENMARK)

*Arctic
Ocean*

*Beaufort
Sea*

ALASKA
(UNITED STATES)

Queen Elizabeth Islands

Quttinirpaaq N.P.

Victoria Island

Baffin Island

*Baffin
Bay*

Sirmilik N.P.

Auyuittuq N.P.

Davis Strait

Aulavik N.P.

Yukon

Queen Charlotte Islands

Tuktut Nogait N.P.

*Great Bear
Lake*

Mackenzie

Mackenzie Mountains

Kluane N.P. & Reserve

Yellowknife

*Great Slave
Lake*

Wood Buffalo N.P.

Athabasca

Peace

*Lake
Athabasca*

Back

Hudson Strait

*Ungava
Peninsula*

*Labrador
Sea*

Labrador

*Hudson
Bay*

Wapusk N.P.

Churchill

Nelson

Saskatchewan

Edmonton

G R E A T   P L A I N S

Jasper N.P.

Banff N.P.

Calgary

R O C K Y   M O U N T A I N S

Fraser

Vancouver

Vancouver Island

*Pacific
Ocean*

Riding Mountain N.P.

*Lake
Winnipeg*

Winnipeg

Lake Superior

Lake Michigan

Pukaskwa N.P.

*Lake
Huron*

Toronto

L. Erie

Ottawa ✪ Ottawa

Lake Ontario

Montréal

Québec

La Mauricie N.P.

Laurentian Mountains

St. Lawrence

*Gaspé
Peninsula*

*Gulf of
St. Lawrence*

*Smallwood
Reservoir*

Gros Morne N.P.

Island of Newfoundland

St.-Pierre & Miquelon (FRANCE)

Cape Breton Highlands N.P.

Bay of Fundy

*Atlantic
Ocean*

U N I T E D   S T A T E S

MAP KEY

Primary vegetation zones/ecosystems

Boreal forest

Ice, glaciers

Temperate coniferous forest

Temperate broadleaf forest

Temperate grassland

Tundra

Protected lands

National park

miles   600

km   600

Rolling Prairies

Canada's prairies were once a vast sea of grass crossed by great herds of bison. Today most of the prairies are fields of cereals or crops grown for the oil in their seeds. Farming and hunting had a severe impact on animals, such as pronghorn antelope and bison. They almost died out but are now protected in reserves. The swift fox was hunted for its fur until the last fox in the prairies was killed in 1928. In the 1980s it was reintroduced from the United States to Alberta and Saskatchewan, where it is thriving.

A Green Blanket

Fly over much of Canada and you see an expanse of dark evergreen forests covering almost 800 million

▼ **A snow-capped peak is framed by a vast evergreen forest near Whistler. British Columbia produces half of all Canada's wood products.**

acres (333 million hectares). In the frozen north, there are far fewer trees, mainly birch, fir, and larch, with boggy areas known as muskegs covered by mats of moss.

More varied forests flourish along the Pacific coast and on the slopes of the Rockies. British Columbia's Great Bear Rainforest is the largest area of non-tropical rain forest in the world. It has a much cooler climate than tropical rain forests, although it is just as wet. Some of the forests trees are a thousand years old. The forest is the home of a rare type of black bear—the kermode or spirit bear. About one in ten spirit bears are born with white fur.

▲ Moose, like this one at Maligne Lake, Alberta, have adapted well to human activities.

▼ A First Nations myth says that the gods made spirit bears white as a reminder that the world was once covered in snow.

Canada's national tree, the maple, grows best in the south, like other deciduous trees—or trees that drop their leaves in fall—such as poplar, ash, beech, hickory, and oak. Some people worry that demand for wood is pushing logging deeper into Canada's wild forests. They warn that trees are being cut down so quickly that new ones do not have time to grow and replace them.

Tough on the Tundra

About a quarter of Canada is cold, bare ground known as tundra. Freezing winds scour the thin soil, and few plants can survive apart from mosses, lichens, and small shrubs. Plants grow more slowly here than in any other ecosystem. Reindeer moss, the main food of caribou, grows just ⅛ inch (3 mm) a year. Animals of the tundra must endure the winter, like the shaggy musk ox, or move south, like the caribou.

GIANT OF THE FOREST

Not usually described as handsome, a moose has bulk on its side. The moose is the world's biggest deer, taller than a human and weighing up to 1,400 pounds (640 kg). A bull moose's antlers can be up to 6 feet (1.8 m) across. Mature bulls shed their antlers toward the end of the year and replace them in spring. Female moose do not have antlers. Moose usually live on their own in the forest, where they graze on twigs and water plants. Moose like the water and are excellent swimmers.

◀ A velvet covering, full of blood vessels, nourishes the antlers. When the antlers are grown, the bull scrapes the velvet off.

Beware Bears

Canada's largest bears are the grizzlies and polar bears. But forest park visitors are most likely to meet black bears. Bears are generally shy and avoid humans. When they become used to humans, however, they may create a problem, wandering into tourist campsites looking for food. In this case they have to be captured, sometimes even killed.

Black bears eat a lot in the summer and fall, gaining

up to 14 pounds (30 kilograms) a week as they prepare for a long winter sleep, known as hibernation. Bears can go for as long as 100 days without eating, drinking, excreting, or exercising. In the spring they wake up hungry, having lost up to 40 percent of their weight.

Scientists still do not understand how bears know when it is time to go into or leave their dens. Studying hibernating bears in their dens takes great care: No one wants to wake one up!

▲ **Bears are skilled fishers. This black bear stares intently into the waters of Clayoquot Sound as it watches for salmon.**

THE 5,000-MILE MIGRATION OF THE CARIBOU

One of Canada's most astonishing sights is a herd of caribou on the move. Caribou winter in the southern forests and migrate north onto the tundra for the summer. As the days lengthen and sun warms the soil in spring, pregnant females are the first to head north for the calving grounds. After the calves are born, the caribou wander the tundra looking for fresh grazing. They store fat in their bodies to give them energy for the mating season in the fall and the journey back to the south. Caribou migrate in herds of as many as 500,000 animals. Wolves follow the herd, looking to pick off stragglers or sick animals.

▶ **Caribou swim across the Yukon River. Their hollow winter hair helps them float high in the water. Even the calves can swim well.**

From
Furs
to
Federation

THE ANCESTORS OF THE FIRST NATIONS, the name given to the native people of Canada, arrived during a gradual migration of people across North and South America. For thousands of years human impact on Canada reflected the lives of the First Nation peoples. In the 16th century French and British settlers arrived. They traded and fought with the First Nations. The name Canada dates from this time and is thought to have come from the Iroquois word "kanata," meaning "village." By the 18th century the two rivals were fighting one another. The British won, but French Canada remained a vibrant part of the country. Later immigrants also added their contributions as Canada grew to nationhood.

◄ **Ojibwa Indians, descendants of the First Nations, come together at powwows to dance, sing, visit, renew old friendships, and make new ones.**

EARLY CANADIANS

Historians believe that people first came to Canada across a land bridge that joined Asia and North America between 15,000 and 30,000 years ago. They gradually spread across the country.

Around A.D. 1000 Leif Eriksson reached Newfoundland from Greenland, where Vikings from Scandinavia had settled. He called his discovery Vinland (Wineland), perhaps in the hope that the name would attract other settlers. A few Vikings came, but their settlement did not last.

Time line

This chart shows the approximate dates of important events in Canada's history, from the arrival of the first Europeans to the foundation of the modern nation.

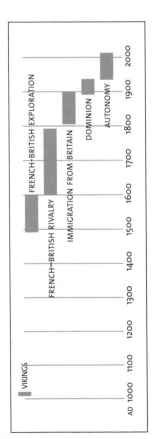

▲ Palisades woven from saplings protect the longhouses of this reconstruction of a 16th-century Iroquoian village at Lawson, Ontario.

Europeans did not return to Canada until John Cabot landed in 1497. Cabot was an Italian hired by the king of England. He returned home with news that the sea teemed with fish, attracting fishers from England and France. Europeans hoped Canada would be rich in gold but instead found a different kind of wealth: fish, timber, and furs.

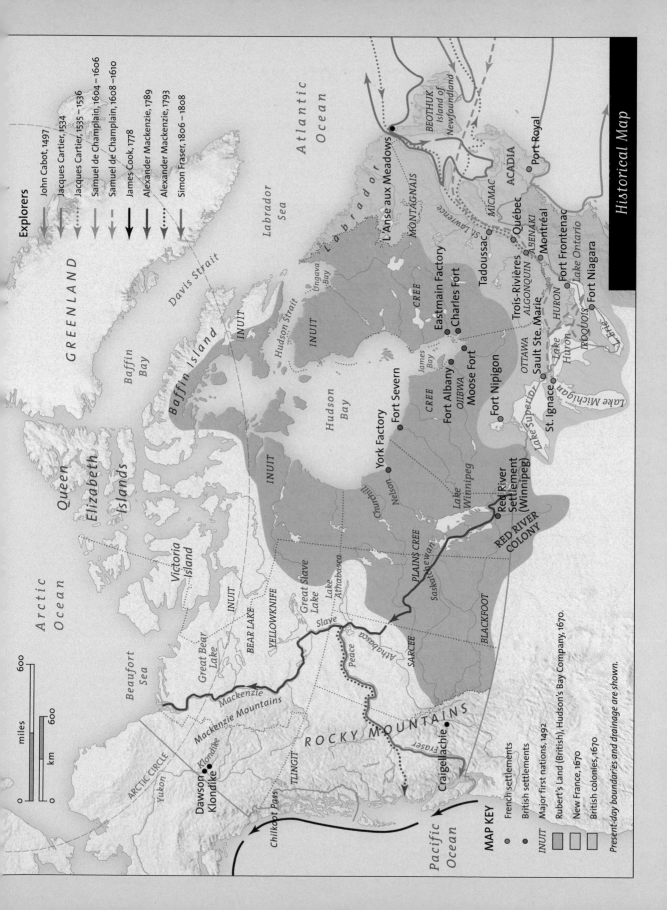

Historical Map

Explorers

→ John Cabot, 1497
→ Jacques Cartier, 1534
⋯→ Jacques Cartier, 1535 – 1536
→ Samuel de Champlain, 1604 – 1606
–→ Samuel de Champlain, 1608 – 1610
→ James Cook, 1778
→ Alexander Mackenzie, 1789
⋯→ Alexander Mackenzie, 1793
→ Simon Fraser, 1806 – 1808

Arctic Ocean

Queen Elizabeth Islands

GREENLAND

Baffin Bay

Beaufort Sea

Victoria Island

Baffin Island

Davis Strait

Labrador Sea

Atlantic Ocean

BEOTHUK
Island of Newfoundland

Mackenzie Mountains

Great Bear Lake

BEAR LAKE

INUIT

YELLOWKNIFE

Great Slave Lake

Slave

Mackenzie

Hudson Strait

Ungava Bay

INUIT

INUIT

INUIT

Hudson Bay

Labrador

L'Anse aux Meadows

MONTAGNAIS

Tadoussac

Québec
Trois-Rivières
Montréal
ABENAKI
ALGONQUIN
Fort Frontenac
Fort Niagara
Lake Ontario
IROQUOIS
Lake Erie

MICMAC
ACADIA
Port Royal

St. Lawrence

Eastmain Factory
Charles Fort

CREE

James Bay
Fort Albany
Moose Fort
OJIBWA
Fort Nipigon
St. Ignace
Sault Ste. Marie
Lake Superior
OTTAWA
HURON
Lake Huron
Lake Michigan

Fort Severn

York Factory

Nelson
Churchill

Lake Winnipeg

Red River Settlement (Winnipeg)
RED RIVER COLONY

PLAINS CREE

CREE

Saskatchewan

Athabasca

Lake Athabasca

Peace

SARCEE

BLACKFOOT

SACREE

ROCKY MOUNTAINS

Fraser

Craigellachie

TLINGIT

Chilkoot Pass

Pacific Ocean

Dawson
Klondike
Klondike
Yukon

ARCTIC CIRCLE

MAP KEY

● French settlements
● British settlements
INUIT Major first nations, 1492
▨ Rubert's Land (British), Hudson's Bay Company, 1670.
▨ New France, 1670
☐ British colonies,1670

Present-day boundaries and drainage are shown.

miles 0 ____ 600
km 0 ____ 600

The First Nations

In the Arctic, small groups of Inuit lived in skin tents in summer and built snow houses in winter. These peoples hunted seals, walrus, caribou, and musk ox. They traveled in sealskin boats or across the snow on sleds pulled by dogs. Superb craftworkers, Inuit made spears, knives, and works of art from the bones and antlers of animals they hunted. Other First Nations peoples, such as the Iroquois of the eastern woodlands, became involved in the French-British wars. The Iroquois also fought their neighbors, the Huron, Cree, and Ojibwa. The Iroquois were farmers as well as hunters, growing corn, beans, and squash, and gathering wild rice. The Europeans moved into lands belonging to the First Nations.

▲ **Two people cross a lake in a traditional birchbark canoe. This type of boat was invented by First Nations people. It was light enough to be carried and ideal for travel on lakes and rivers.**

French and British Rivalry

To find furs, French hunters began exploring inland, traveling on foot and horseback, in boats, on rafts, and in bark canoes like those made by local people. The French started a colony in Canada, called New France, and founded settlements at Acadia, Quebec, and Montreal. They made allies of the Huron and other First Nations people to help them fight the powerful Iroquois nation. French missionary-priests taught the Christian religion and started the first churches in Canada.

While the French were settling eastern Canada and pushing south along the Mississippi River into what is now the United States, the British explored around Hudson Bay, named for Henry Hudson, who sailed there in 1610. The centuries-old rivalry between France and Britain in Europe made disputes likely as British farmers and French fur traders competed for land. There were four wars between 1689 and 1763 for control of North America, fought by colonists, soldiers, and sailors from Europe, and also by First Nations peoples. The last war, the Seven Years' War (also called the French and Indian War), ended in 1763 with Britain winning control of Canada.

▲ Tourists visit L'Anse aux Meadows in Newfoundland, settled by Vikings around 1000.

▼ The green-turreted Chateau Frontenac in Quebec City, now a hotel, is named after a governor of New France.

Canada Grows

By the 18th century, in addition to governing Canada as a colony, Britain had 13 colonies to the south in what is now the United States. When American colonists fought and won the

A COUNTRY BUILT ON FUR

The fur trade was very important in Canada's early history. French trappers opened up new routes along Canada's rivers, trading tools and weapons for furs with the First Nations peoples they met, and exchanging furs for supplies at trading posts. In 1670 the English Hudson's Bay Company began shipping thousands of beaver furs to Europe to be made into winter coats and waterproof felt for men's hats. The fur trade prospered until the mid-1800s, when silk hats came into fashion.

Revolutionary War (1775–1783), thousands of Loyalists who did not wish to live in the new republic moved north to settle in Canada.

In 1791 Britain split the growing colony into Upper (British) and Lower (French) Canada. As settlers and explorers traveled west, Canada was growing steadily larger, gaining new territories such as the Red River Colony (mainly in what is now Manitoba) in 1812, and British Columbia in 1848. In 1812 the population was still less than 100,000, but by the 1860s it had topped three million and was still growing fast as new immigrants arrived, mostly from Britain.

▼ This reconstruction shows how fur traders built homes within palisades for protection.

War and Rebellion

In 1812 war broke out between the United States and Britain. American forces invaded Canada but were stopped by a small force of British soldiers, helped by fur traders, First Nations people, and Loyalists, who no longer felt any allegiance to their former country.

Their success helped create a feeling of common identity against the invaders.

Even so, some French Canadians were unhappy. And First Nations leaders did not want to see their land being taken over by settlers. In 1837 a French Canadian named Louis Papineau led an unsuccessful rebellion against the British authorities in Lower Canada.

In 1867 Upper and Lower Canada became Ontario and Quebec. They were combined with Nova Scotia and New Brunswick to form a dominion with its own government, parliament, and prime minister.

The Métis of Red River Colony objected to being made part of the dominion. They were afraid that settlers from Ontario would take their land. In 1869, Louis Riel led an uprising and took control of the colony. He made sure that when the Red River Colony became part of Canada in 1870, it was on fair terms. As a result of Riel's negotiations, the colony joined as part of the new province of Manitoba. As in Quebec,

THE MÉTIS

French trappers often married First Nations women; their children were known as Métis (may-tees). Métis were buffalo hunters, fur traders, and farmers. They spoke a language that was a mixture of French and Cree. Canadians who have part-French, part-First Nations ancestry still use the term to describe themselves.

▼ Reenactors in period costume celebrate the British victories in the War of 1812. British forces even occupied the U.S. capital, Washington, D.C.

English and French (the Métis' language) were given equal status in Manitoba. Riel was forced into exile in the United States in 1875. In 1885 Riel led First Nations and Métis in a similar revolt, in what is now part of Saskatchewan. This time he was captured and executed in Regina as a traitor. In Quebec, however, Riel was seen as a hero.

The Mounties

As settlers built homes, farms, and towns in the wilderness, law and order were maintained by the North-West Mounted Police, nicknamed the Mounties. Their first task in 1873 was to prevent fighting between First Nations tribes and whiskey smugglers from the United States. The First Nations respected the Mounties, who treated them fairly.

▲ Louis Riel led the Métis of the Northwest in their resistance against the Canadian government. Statues of Riel now stand on Parliament Hill in Ottawa and outside the provincial legislature in Winnipeg, Manitoba.

The Mounties also played an important role in keeping the peace in 1877, when Sitting Bull led thousands of Sioux into Canada from the United States. The Plains tribes had defeated General Custer and the U.S. 7th Cavalry at the Battle of the Little Bighorn. Mountie commander James Morrow Walsh met Sitting Bull with fewer than 100 men, but he persuaded the Sioux leader to obey the laws of the "Great White Mother" (Queen Victoria).

The Mounties built up an international reputation for always "getting their man." In 1904 King Edward VII added "Royal" to their name. In 1920 they became the Royal Canadian Mounted Police.

A SEA ROUTE TO ASIA

When Europeans began trading with Asia by sea, ships had to make the long voyage around Africa to reach the East. Geographers suggested it might be quicker to sail west, and find a northwest passage to the Pacific Ocean through Canada's rivers and the Arctic ice. For 300 years explorers, among them Martin Frobisher, Henry Hudson, and Sir John Franklin, searched in vain. In 1906 Roald Amundsen of Norway in his yacht *Gjoa* finally completed the epic voyage through the ice from the Atlantic to the Pacific Ocean.

▲ A cross commemorates the 135 men who lost their lives on Sir John Franklin's 1845 expedition.

The Railroad Spans a Nation

In the 19th century a transportation revolution helped unite Canada. On November 7, 1885, the eastern and western sections of the Canadian Pacific Railway met at Craigellachie, British Columbia, six years ahead of

▼ Explorers trying to find the Northwest Passage had to navigate through jagged sheets of ice like these.

▲ A train winds along the Bow River. The railroad opened western Canada to settlers and visitors from the east.

schedule, linking Canada's populated areas with the relatively unpopulated west. The new railroad helped speed the development of the western provinces.

KLONDIKE GOLD RUSH

In 1896 prospectors struck gold in the Klondike River, Yukon Territory. The following year thousands of gold-crazy fortune hunters were heading north for the backbreaking climb over the Chilkoot Pass into Canada. Boomtowns like Dawson mushroomed into rough-and-ready life in a few weeks. Few of the Klondikers made their fortunes, and many lost their lives. Those who survived went home tougher, wiser, and with many tales to tell.

Modern Canada

In 1931 Canada became an independent nation. The current British monarch, Queen Elizabeth II, is the head of state, but she has purely ceremonial duties.

In the 1960s a French-Canadian group campaigned for Quebec to leave Canada. Independence was rejected by Quebec's voters in 1980 and again in 1995.

First Nations groups also campaigned for greater equality and land rights. Since the 1980s

First Nations people have been granted increasing self-government. In 1999 the traditional lands of the Inuit were made into the new territory of Nunavut.

Meanwhile, Canada played a leading role in international affairs. Its forces fought with Britain and the United States in World War I (1914–1918) and World War II (1939–1945). Canada became a key member of the United Nations (UN) and the North Atlantic Treaty Organization (NATO). Its troops joined UN forces in the Korean War (1950–1953) and took part in peace-keeping operations around the world.

Canada staged the Montreal World's Fair, Expo 67, in 1967 and the Olympic Games, also in Montreal, in 1976. The events attracted many visitors, and much praise, from around the world.

In the first decade of the 21st century, Canada is firmly established on the world stage. Despite the powerful influence of its neighbor, the United States, Canada has developed its own distinctive cultural, economic, and political identity.

▼ Canadian troops shelter from shells in northern France during World War II.

Many Nations *in* One

I N SOME WAYS CANADA is many nations in one. Descendants of British and French immigrants make up about half the population, reflecting the history of the country. They were followed by other European and Asian immigrants. New immigrants tended to settle in particular places and keep their traditions. Many Dutch, for example, settled in Ontario, where the flat, fertile land was similar to the Netherlands and where they could grow fruit and vegetables as they had done at home. Other groups, such as the Chinese, made their homes in specific areas of Toronto, Montreal, and Vancouver. The First Nations, who arrived thousands of years before the British and French, make up about 4 percent of the current population. Together these diverse peoples have created a distinctively Canadian culture.

◀ Hot-air balloons illustrate sources of pride for many Canadians: the flag, the maple leaf, and the Mounties, Canada's mounted police force.

MULTICULTURAL CANADA

Canada is a nation of immigrants. Arrivals from other countries shaped its history and the country still accepts 250,000 immigrants every year. In the early decades of European settlement, most new arrivals were from France and Britain. They were joined after the American Revolution (1775–1783) by Loyalists from the United States. In the 19th and early 20th centuries, the Canadian government encouraged immigrants to work in agriculture and industry, including people from the Balkans in southeastern Europe and Chinese workers who built the railroads.

Some Canadians feared for their own jobs and ways of life. In the 1920s, laws excluded immigrants from Asia and other regions. The laws were replaced in the 1960s by new laws that still operate today, which encourage immigration and the creation of a multicultural society. Many new arrivals in Canada are South and East Asian s, with valuable skills in computing and other high-technology areas. But for every four immigrants that arrive, Canada loses one emigrant. Professionals often move to the United States, where wages are higher.

Common Canadian Phrases

Canadian use many of the same everyday phrases and greetings as Americans and Britons, but with local variations. Here are a few local expressions:

Chucklehead (Newfoundland)	Stupid person
Cheechako (Yukon)	Newcomer
Autoroute (Quebec)	Highway
Loonie	Dollar coin
Toonie	Two-dollar coin
Hydro	Electricity
Runners	Sneakers

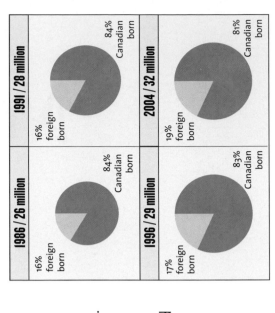

1986 / 26 million — 16% foreign born, 84% Canadian born

1991 / 28 million — 16% foreign born, 84% Canadian born

1996 / 29 million — 17% foreign born, 83% Canadian born

2004 / 32 million — 19% foreign born, 81% Canadian born

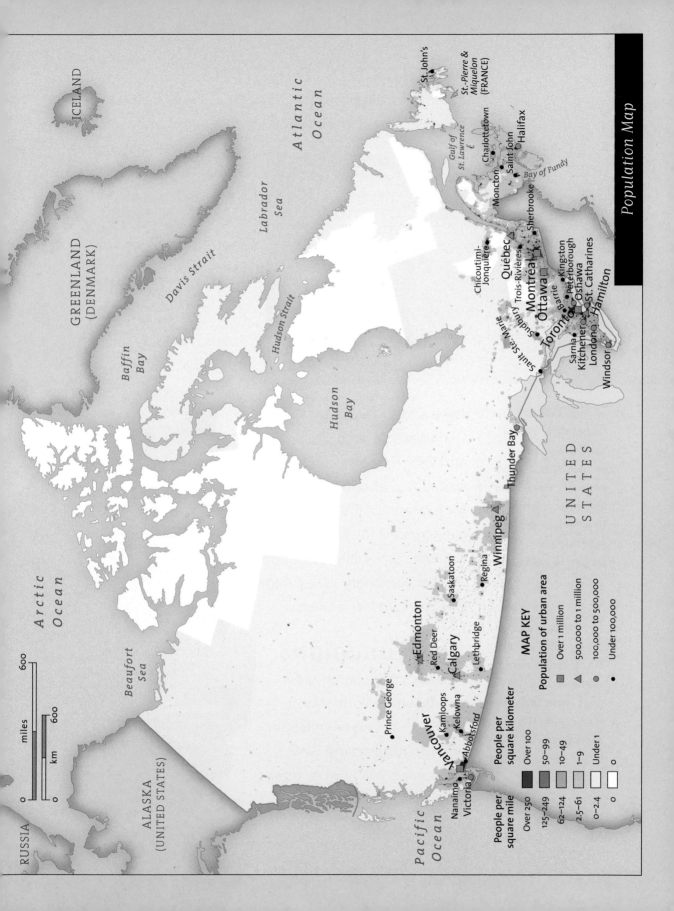

Population Map

RUSSIA

Arctic Ocean

ICELAND

GREENLAND
(DENMARK)

ALASKA
(UNITED STATES)

Beaufort Sea

Baffin
Bay

Davis Strait

Labrador Sea

Atlantic Ocean

Hudson Strait

Hudson
Bay

Pacific Ocean

Prince George

Kamloops
Kelowna
Nanaimo
Victoria
Vancouver
Abbotsford

Edmonton
Red Deer
Calgary
Lethbridge

Saskatoon

Regina

Winnipeg

Thunder Bay

UNITED
STATES

Sault Ste. Marie

Sudbury

Barrie
Peterborough
Oshawa

Toronto
Hamilton
St. Catharines
Kitchener
London
Windsor
Sarnia

Kingston

Ottawa
Montréal
Trois-Rivières
Québec
Chicoutimi-
Jonquière

Sherbrooke

Moncton

Charlottetown
Saint John
Halifax

Bay of Fundy

*Gulf of
St. Lawrence*

St. John's

*St.-Pierre &
Miquelon
(FRANCE)*

MAP KEY

**People per
square kilometer**

Over 100
50–99
10–49
1–9
Under 1

Population of urban area

☐ Over 1 million
△ 500,000 to 1 million
● 100,000 to 500,000
• Under 100,000

**People per
square mile**

Over 250
125–249
62–124
2.5–61
0–2.4

miles   600

km   600

Keeping up Traditions

Canadians, whatever their ancestry, like to maintain old customs. Scots celebrate Burns Night and wear kilts, and Irish celebrate St. Patrick's Day. Others are proud of their French connections or keep up traditions their forefathers brought from Germany, Scandinavia, Italy, Poland, Ukraine, and other parts of Europe,

▲ Many Inuit still follow their traditional way of life, which includes building igloos, temporary winter homes used on hunting trips, from blocks of snow. A small hole at the top provides ventilation.

▶ The figures on a totem pole are a record of First Nations myth and history, and each group has its own style of decoration. This one was carved by the Sechelt Band of British Columbia.

Asia, and the Caribbean. Canadians of both Caribbean and British backgrounds are passionate about cricket, for example. Americans, too, crossed the border into Canada, especially during and after the Revolutionary War, bringing thier customs with them.

New Canadians

Canada's population grew rapidly after World War II (1939–1945), when millions of migrants became new Canadians. Many were from

Europe, but others came from China, India, Pakistan, Africa, and Latin America. Refugees fled from troublespots such as Hungary in 1956 and from Vietnam and Cambodia in the 1970s. In the 21st century, most new Canadians have come from Asia, chiefly from India and the Philippines.

Old Canadians

Inuit people live mostly in the Northwest Territories and Nunavut, or in northern Labrador, Ontario, and Quebec. Never call an Inuit an Eskimo; in their language the word means "eaters of raw meat." Most Native Americans prefer to be known as members of a tribal group, such as the Objibwa of Ontario or the Cree of Quebec.

Many Native Americans live on their traditional lands, but others have moved to cities across Canada. Some practice traditional skills—the people of the Pacific coast, for example, make ceremonial masks with startling, painted faces, and carve tall totem poles. First Nations sculptures, paintings, and dances have become widely recognized and popular symbols of Canadian culture.

THE CALGARY STAMPEDE

The Stampede is held every July, at Calgary in Alberta. Fans flock to watch bull riding, steer roping, bareback horse riding, and the thrilling chuck-wagon race, with its spectacular crashes. The event also features street fairs, a First Nations village, and a replica frontier town recalling Canada's Wild West days.

▶ **Chuck-wagon riders round a corner at breakneck speed.**

▼ **A snowboarder flies through the air at Mount Norquay in Alberta.**

A Nation of Sports Fans

Canadians' favorite game is hockey, and there are ice rinks in most towns. Canada's big cities support professional teams, such as the Calgary Flames, who compete in the National Hockey League (NHL) with U.S. teams and vie for the prestigious Stanley Cup. The Montreal Canadiens still hold the record of five straight Stanley Cup championships between 1956 and 1960. One of the sport's best known players was Canadian Wayne Gretzky, a star in the NHL between 1979 and 1999. Nicknamed "the Great One," he held 61 NHL records when he retired; his famed No. 99 was retired with him.

The Moosomin Moose Hockey Team of Moosomin, Saskatchewan, set an unusual record in 2003, when they played the longest hockey game ever, lasting 62 hours and 15 minutes.

Canada's national men's hockey team has been world champion more than 20 times, and the Canadian women's team has dominated the women's world championships since they began in 1990.

Canadians enjoy winter sports, and winter slopes are full of skiers and snowboarders. Fans also take to the outdoors for snowmobiling. Curling, which involves sliding heavy "stones" across ice, is also popular. People skate outdoors, under floodlights, before warming up with hot snacks and drinks.

▲ Children play hockey in the icy streets of Inuvik in the Northwest Territories.

NATIONAL HOLIDAYS

Canadians have 10 national holidays, but the territories and provinces celebrate their own additional holidays.

JANUARY 1	New Year's Day
MARCH/APRIL	Good Friday
	Easter Sunday
	Easter Monday
MONDAY BEFORE MAY 25	Victoria Day
JULY 1	Canada Day
FIRST MONDAY IN SEPTEMBER	Labor Day
SECOND MONDAY IN OCTOBER	Thanksgiving Day
NOVEMBER 11	Remembrance Day
DECEMBER 25	Christmas Day
DECEMBER 26	Boxing Day

▼ The CN Tower and the Toronto skyline at night

Canadians also play baseball and Canadian football, which is like American football, but with a different scoring system. Soccer is growing in popularity, particularly among young people. In the summer, golf, tennis, and cricket are popular.

Arts and Literature

Canadian arts and media were slow to develop because communities were scattered, but in the 1970s the government passed laws encouraging Canadian material in television and radio shows. Today Canadian music, dance, film, theater, and literature have an international audience. Writers such as Margaret Atwood and Saul Bellow are world figures. The Group of Seven were influential landscape artists based in Ontario in the 1920s. Singer Céline Dion was brought up in rural Quebec and began her singing career in French. She only learned English at age 18 and went on to sell 100 million albums.

The most dramatic example of Canadian architecture is Toronto's CN Tower. The world's tallest free-standing structure, it is 1,815 feet (553 meters) to the top. The record for climbing the 1,776 steps is under eight minutes. On a windy day, the tower actually sways!

LIFE IN NUNAVUT

In far northern Nunavut, the sun never sets in midsummer—this is the land of the midnight sun. A quarter of Nunavut, Canada's newest territory, is made up by Baffin Island, mountainous, bare of trees, and bitterly cold in winter. Here hardy visitors can hike, paddle a kayak, or try dogsledding and snowmobiling. Inuit people live throughout Canada, but most still prefer life in Nunavut, which means "our land." In spring, the Inuit base themselves in camps from where they set out on hunting and fishing trips. During shorter expeditions in winter, they may build temporary snow houses.

▲ An Inuit woman hoists a carcass onto her shoulders at a hunting camp near Baker Lake.

Flavors of Canada

Canada's many immigrants brought their food traditions with them. When combined with local ingredients, the results are some special dishes. Visitors to the prairies can enjoy saskatoon berry pie made with sweet, purple berries called saskatoons, while a visit to Quebec City gives a taste of French cooking with a Canadian twist in recipes such as chicken breasts baked in maple syrup. In the north, moose sausages or caribou steak may be on the menu, while a tomato and coconut curry with fish, crabs, and mussels is just one of the dishes that has given Vancouver a reputation for the country's best Indian and Chinese food.

A Wealthy Nation

THE DIVISION THAT LIES at the heart of Canada dates back to the 1600s when France established a colony centered on Quebec. When Britain challenged France's supremacy in Canada, years of rivalry and conflict followed. Britain won but, in the Quebec Act of 1774, granted the people of Quebec their own legal and religious rights. The differences between French and English Canada led to the growth of a separatist movement in Quebec that demanded an independent French-speaking nation. In two polls held in 1980 and 1995, Quebec citizens voted to remain within the federation. But the second vote was very close. And although Canada entered the 21st century as a united nation, Quebec's dream of independence has not died.

◀ Demonstrators express their views at a rally in Montreal before Quebecers went to the polls in 1995 to vote on whether Quebec should split from Canada.

THE FEDERATION

Canada is a federation of 13 provinces and territories. There are ten provinces: Newfoundland and Labrador, Nova Scotia, Prince Edward Island, New Brunswick, Quebec, Ontario, Manitoba, Saskatchewan, Alberta, and British Columbia. There are also three territories: the Northwest Territories, Yukon, and Nunavut (see political map opposite). Each province has its own capital, government, and premier, while the federal government in Ottawa deals with matters that affect all Canadians, such as defense and foreign policy.

Each province has an appointed lieutenant-governor with ceremonial powers only. An elected assembly and government, led by a premier, look after provincial matters such as education, justice, civil rights, and income and property taxes. Smaller councils run counties, districts, cities, townships, and villages. A federal minister for Indian Affairs and Northern Development heads programs intended to benefit First Nations groups.

▲ **Wheat fields surround a farm in Saskatchewan. Canada produces about 20 percent of the world's wheat exports, mainly for Japan and China.**

Trading Partners

The majority of Canada's exports go to the United States, but it also exports wheat to Asia and manufactured goods to Europe. Among its chief exports are motor vehicles, industrial machinery, and chemicals. Imports include oil, chemicals, and consumer goods.

Country	Percent Canada Exports
United States	84.2%
Japan	2.1%
United Kingdom	1.8%
All others combined	11.9%

Country	Percent Canada Imports
United States	56.7%
China	7.8%
Mexico	3.8%
All others combined	31.7%

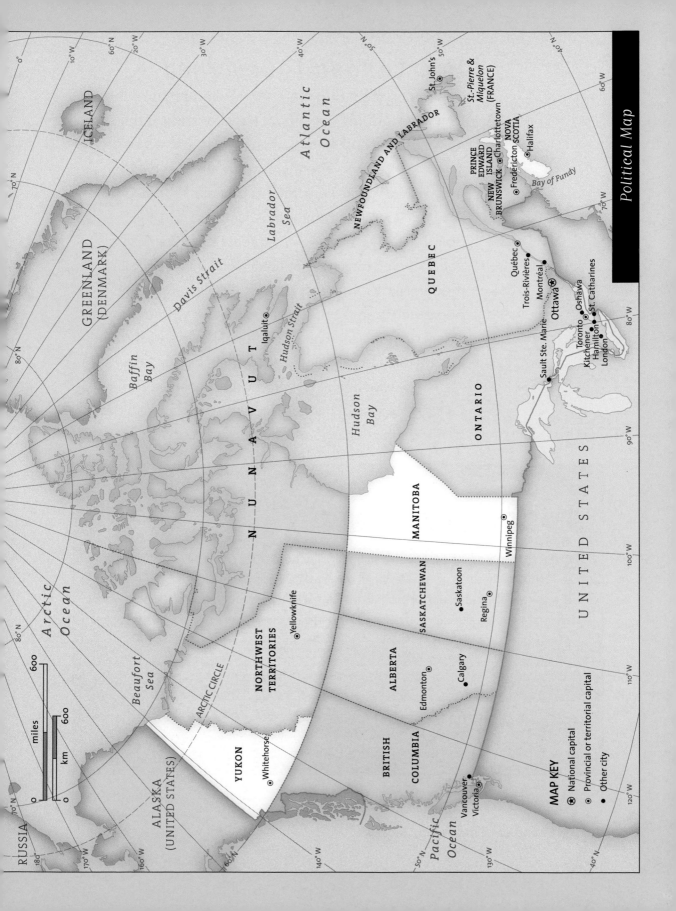

Political Map

MAP KEY
⊛ National capital
⊙ Provincial or territorial capital
● Other city

RUSSIA

ALASKA
(UNITED STATES)

Arctic Ocean

Beaufort Sea

Pacific Ocean

YUKON
⊙ Whitehorse

ARCTIC CIRCLE

NORTHWEST TERRITORIES
⊙ Yellowknife

BRITISH COLUMBIA

Vancouver ●
Victoria ⊙

ALBERTA
Edmonton ⊙
Calgary ●

SASKATCHEWAN
● Saskatoon
Regina ⊙

MANITOBA
Winnipeg ⊙

NUNAVUT

Iqaluit ⊙

Baffin Bay

Davis Strait

Hudson Strait

Hudson Bay

GREENLAND (DENMARK)

ICELAND

Labrador Sea

NEWFOUNDLAND AND LABRADOR

St. John's ●

St-Pierre & Miquelon (FRANCE)

QUEBEC

Québec ⊙
Trois-Rivières ●
Montréal ●
Ottawa ⊛

ONTARIO

Sault Ste. Marie ●
Toronto ⊙
Oshawa ●
Kitchener ●
Hamilton ●
London ●
St. Catharines ●

PRINCE EDWARD ISLAND
Charlottetown ⊙

NEW BRUNSWICK
Fredericton ⊙

NOVA SCOTIA
● Halifax

Bay of Fundy

Atlantic Ocean

UNITED STATES

miles 0 ___ 600
km 0 ___ 600

How Canada Is Governed

Canada's system of government follows that of the United Kingdom. The official head of state is the ruling monarch of Britain, who is represented by the governor-general. The governor-general serves for five years and has very limited powers.

The federal government is formed from the political party that wins most seats in parliament at national elections held at least every five years. In modern times the most powerful political parties have been the Liberals and Progressive Conservatives, with smaller parties such as the Reform Party and the Bloc Québécois also having sizeable backing.

The leader of the governing party serves as Canada's prime minister. He or she heads a cabinet of ministers in charge of government departments.

HOW THE GOVERNMENT WORKS

The British monarch is the head of state, but since Queen Elizabeth II only visits Canada occasionally, she is represented by an appointed Canadian governor-general. Effective power and decision-making rest with the elected federal government, which makes laws by passing bills through parliament. The Prime Minister heads the government and appoints judges.

QUEEN/GOVERNOR-GENERAL				
EXECUTIVE	LEGISLATIVE		JUDICIARY	
PRIME MINISTER	PARLIAMENT		SUPREME COURT	
CABINET (APPOINTED BY PRIME MINISTER)	SENATE 104 MEMBERS	HOUSE OF COMMONS 301 MEMBERS	FEDERAL COURT	

Rewards for Hard Work

Canada has huge natural resources: forests, minerals, water power, fertile soils, and a skilled workforce. The biggest group of workers are employed in service industries, such as finance, stores, hotels, and restaurants. Other important employers are mining and transportation.

Canada is a rich nation. More than 60 percent of households have at least one car, almost everyone has a television, and about half have a home computer.

▲ The world's largest shopping mall, in West Edmonton, contains a replica of the *Santa Maria* of Christopher Columbus.

▼ The Centennial Flame outside the Parliament Buildings in Ottawa was lit in 1967 to celebrate the country's 100th birthday.

Farming, Fishing, and Forestry

Less than one-twelfth of Canada is suitable for farming, and only 4 percent of the population work on farms. Although there are not many of them, Canada's farmers produce a lot of food—around 15 million tons of wheat and 9 million tons of corn a year. They also grow other grains, and vegetables such as potatoes, tomatoes, carrots, onions, cabbage, and soybeans. Canadian farms support about 14 million cows— that's roughly one cow to every two people in the country.

▲ Rivers are a great way to deliver logs to lumber and paper mills.

Fishing was once Canada's biggest industry. When John Cabot reached Newfoundland 500 years ago, he joked that the cod were so thick that he could walk across their backs to the shore. His sailors scooped the fish up in buckets. For centuries Canadian fishers made their living from cod, but 20th-century fishing methods led to overfishing, and the industry collapsed. Today there are strict limits on catches of Atlantic cod.

The Pacific salmon is vital to the economy of British Columbia. Most commercial catches end up in cans, but anglers from all over the world also come to British Columbia to try to catch a wild Pacific salmon. Pacific salmon

THE WOMAN WHO SAVED THE WHEAT

Margaret Newton was one of the first women to study science in Canada. She was at college in 1916 when a disease called rust devastated the wheat harvest. Newton discovered that there were different kinds of rust. Her breakthrough enabled experts to breed wheat that resisted the disease. There has been no serious outbreak on the prairies since the 1950s. By the time Newton died in 1971, she was one of the leading wheat experts not just in Canada but throughout the world.

LEGENDARY LUMBERJACKS

Many tall tales are told about Canada's early lumberjacks. They lived in logging camps in the forests, felling trees with axes and saws and taking the logs to mills with a team of oxen or rafting them down rivers. It was dangerous, lonely work. On long, winter nights they sat around the fire telling stories. Almost every man knew a jack who could saw faster, roll a log quicker, or climb a tree higher than any other logger alive. Today such skills are kept alive in lumberjack games where contestants roll logs, cut logs with axes or saws, or throw axes.

▶ A lumberjack takes part in a competition that includes sawing and tree climbing.

return to the rivers of their birth to spawn and die. Scientists still do not fully understand how they find their way. About every four years Canada is home to one of nature's most remarkable sights. As many as two million sockeye salmon make their way up the Fraser River, past hydroelectric dams, up fishways, and over waterfalls to reach the Adams River, 300 miles (480 kilometers) from the ocean.

Over half of Canada's land is covered with forest, and Canada is the world's leading exporter of pulp and paper. Lumber is also an important export. Responsible

▼ Sockeye salmon swim together to reduce drag from the water.

INDUSTRY

This map shows Canada's main centers for industry, mining, and manufacturing. The most important industrial regions are in Ontario.

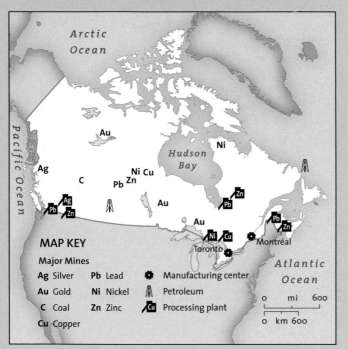

Arctic Ocean

Pacific Ocean

Au

Ni

Hudson Bay

Ag

Ni Cu

C

Pb Zn

Zn

Au

Pb

Au

Pb Zn

Ni Cu

Montréal

Toronto

Atlantic Ocean

MAP KEY

Major Mines

Ag Silver   Pb Lead   ✿ Manufacturing center

Au Gold   Ni Nickel   ⛏ Petroleum

C Coal   Zn Zinc   Cu Processing plant

Cu Copper

0   mi   600

0   km 600

management of Canada's trees is hugely important to wildlife, water supplies, the economy, and the people who work and live in—or visit—the forests.

Getting Around

Canada's huge distances and wilderness areas have always made it tough to get around. First the rivers and then the railroads provided a vital transportation network, and boats and trains still play an important role. Today Canadians use their automobiles a lot, especially in rural areas, and almost 81 percent of Canadians drive to work. There are more than 12 million cars—nearly one for every two Canadians.

Airplanes are the best way to get around quickly, especially in the north where there are few roads. Light aircraft take tourists to remote fishing or hunting lodges, deliver supplies, and save lives in medical emergencies. Many have floats so they can land on lakes. Two-thirds of Canada's more than 66,000 airplane and helicopter pilots fly private aircraft.

Number 1 Internationally

Canada faces a number of possible problems. Visitors to the wilderness may damage the world they come to see. Loggers want to fell more remote forests. Industry faces competition from nations such as China. Some of the best educated Canadians are leaving to work in the United States. The birth rate is so low that population growth relies on immigration.

The Canadians plan to manage their resources better and to keep attracting immigrants with skills that will help the economy. Many people find Canada attractive—and not just Canadians. Every year the United Nations lists the best countries to live in, ranked by factors such as income, quality of housing, crime rates, and access to leisure facilities. Canada has topped the list more than any other nation. Canadians are confident that they can keep up their record.

▼ A seaplane readies for take off from Cli Lake, Northwest Territories. Seaplanes are the best way of getting around in some places—commuters use them and some restaurants even have seaplane parking areas.

Add a Little Extra to Your Country Report!

If you are assigned to write a report about Canada, you'll want to include basic information about the country, of course. The Fast Facts chart on page 8 will give you a good start. The rest of the book will give you the details you need to create a full and up-to-date paper or PowerPoint presentation. But what can you do to make your report more fun than anyone else's? If you use your imagination and dig a bit deeper into some of the topics introduced in this book, you're sure to come up with information that will make your report unique!

>Flag

Perhaps you could explain the history of Canada's flag, and the meanings of its colors and symbols. Go to **www.crwflags.com/fotw/flags** for more information.

>National Anthem

How about downloading Canada's national anthem and playing it for your class? At **www.nationalanthems.info** you'll find what you need, including the words to the anthem, plus sheet music for the anthem. Simply pick "C" and then "Canada" from the list on the left-hand side of the screen, and you're on your way.

>Time Difference

If you want to understand the time difference between Canada and where you are, this Web site can help: **www.worldtimeserver.com**. Just pick a location in Canada from the list on the left. If you called a city in Canada right now, would you wake whomever you are calling from their sleep?

>Currency

Another Web site will convert your money into Canadian dollars, the currency used in Canada. You'll want to know how much money to bring if you're ever lucky enough to travel to Canada: **www.xe.com/ucc**.

>Weather

Why not check the current weather in Canada? It's easy—simply go to **www.weather.com** to find out if it's sunny or cloudy, warm or cold in Canada right this minute! Pick "World" from the headings at the top of the page. Then search for Canada. Click on any city you like. Be sure to click on the tabs below the weather report for Sunrise/Sunset information, Weather Watch, and Business Travel Outlook, too. Scroll down the page for the 36-hour Forecast and a satellite weather map. Compare your weather to the weather in the Canadian city you chose. Is this a good season, weather-wise, for a person to travel to Canada?

>Miscellaneous

Still want more information? Simply go to National Geographic's One-Stop Research site at **http://www.nationalgeographic.com/onestop**. It will help you find maps, photos and art, articles and information, games and features that you can use to jazz up your report.

Glossary

Circumference the distance around the outside of a circle or sphere.

Citadel a fortress built to command a city, often located on a hill or another high point.

Diversity many different plants, animals, or people all living together.

Dominion a country that belongs to the British Commonwealth and whose head of state is the British monarch.

Endangered an animal or plant that is at risk of dying out.

Federation a nation formed by uniting several smaller units, such as Canada's provinces and territories.

Governor-general someone who governs a territory on behalf of a more senior ruler.

Grain elevator a tall building for storing grain.

Ice Age a period when the Earth was colder than it is now and ice covered continents in the north and south.

Ice-bound a river that is frozen.

Loyalists Americans who fought for the British during the American Revolution. Many later settled in Canada.

Migration the annual movement of animals, such as birds, deer, or whales, from one place to another.

Multicultural reflecting the influences of many different cultures.

Muskeg a mossy bog.

Natural resources things in the natural world with an economic value, such as fish, timber, coal, or rivers to generate hydroelectricity.

Overfishing catching so many fish in one place that they do not have the chance to breed, so their numbers fall.

Peace-keeping force a military force from a range of countries sent into troublespots to prevent violence, such as wars.

Prairies areas of largely treeless, generally flat grassland.

Pulp material made from pulverized wood that is used for making paper and other products.

Rodeo a competition of cowboy skills, such as bronco riding and lassoing calves.

Separatist someone who wants their region to be independent rather than part of another country.

Shield in geography, the oldest rocks forming a continent.

Snowmobile a vehicle with skis and tracks for carrying one or two people over snowy ground.

Species a type of organism; animals or plants in the same species look similar and can only breed successfully among themselves.

Subarctic a cold region along the southern fringe of the Arctic.

Totem pole a tall piece of wood carved with human or animal figures to display the history of a particular Native American or First Nation clan.

Trapper a hunter who catches animals for their fur.

Tundra a treeless subarctic plain in which the ground is permanently frozen.

Wilderness a region that has not been disturbed by human beings.

Bibliography

Cheng, Pang Guek. *Culture Shock: Canada*. Portland, OR: Graphic Arts Center Publishing Company, 2006.

Morton, Desmond. *A Short History of Canada*. Toronto: McClelland and Stewart, 2001.

http://atlas.nrcan.gc.ca/site/english/maps/reference (*The Atlas of Canada* from Natural Resources Canada)

http://history.cbc.ca/histicons/ (*Canada: A People's History* from the Canadian Broadcasting Company)

http://www.thecanadianencyclopedia.com (*Historica Canadian Encyclopedia* online)

http://www.pc.gc.ca/ Parks Canada official page

Further Information

NATIONAL GEOGRAPHIC Articles

Eliot, John L. "Refuge in White: Winter in a Canadian National Park." NATIONAL GEOGRAPHIC (December 2005): 46–57.

Gadd, Ben. "Alberta's Untamed Canadian Rockies." NATIONAL GEOGRAPHIC ADVENTURE (May/June 2000): 116–118.

Johnston, Jessie. "Buying Native Art in B.C." NATIONAL GEOGRAPHIC TRAVELER (July/August 2006): 33.

Kadushin, Raphael. "A Tasty Taste of Montreal." NATIONAL GEOGRAPHIC TRAVELER (March 1999): 46–50.

Lange, Karen L. "They Can't Go Home Again." NATIONAL GEOGRAPHIC (March 2003): Geographica.

Mandel, Peter. "Ice Hotel." NATIONAL GEOGRAPHIC KIDS (February 2006): 28–30.

"Parks Special '06: The Best of the Great Parks: Action Plans, Classic Lodges, Secret Corners." NATIONAL GEOGRAPHIC ADVENTURE (June/July 2006): 70–80, 82, 84, 86–90, 92, 107–108.

Peck, Barbara. "Canada Coast-to-Coast." NATIONAL GEOGRAPHIC TRAVELER (November/December 2004): 60–75.

Stren, Olivia. "A Fairy-Tale City." NATIONAL GEOGRAPHIC TRAVELER (October 2006): 50–55.

Vangelova, Luba. "Techies in the Wilderness." NATIONAL GEOGRAPHIC TRAVELER (March 2002): 107–109.

Web sites to explore

More fast facts about Canada, from the CIA (Central Intelligence Agency): https://www.cia.gov/cia/publications/factbook/geos/ca.html

Want to know more about Canada's First Nations? The ministry for Indian and Northern Affairs has a special kids' site: http://www.ainc-inac.gc.ca/ks/index_e.html

Everything you need to know about the Mounties. Click on "About the RCMP": http://www.rcmp-grc.gc.ca/index_e.htm

Interested in Canada's wildlife? Environment Canada is the best place to start: http://www.ns.ec.gc.ca/wildlife/index.html

Index

Credits

Picture Credits

Front Cover- Spine: Richard Nowitz/NGIC; Top: William Albert Allard/NGIC; Lo far left: George F. Mobley/NGIC; Lo left: Theo Allofs/Zefa/Corbis; Lo right: Jim Richardson/NGIC; Lo far right: Paul Nicklen/NGIC.

Interior—Corbis: 34 up; Richard Hamilton-Smith: 30 up; Hulton Deutsch Collection: 37 lo; Brooks Kraft: 3 right, 48-49; Gunter Marx Photography: 55 up; Tom Nebbia: 25 lo; NG Image Collection: William Albert Allard: 44 up; James P. Blair: 32 lo; Richard Alexander Cooke III: 28 up; Mark Cosslett: 44 lo; Raymond Gehman: 2 right, 5 up, 16 lo, 18-19, 22 lo, 24 center, 36 up, 54 up, 57 lo; Taylor S. Kennedy: 59 up; Emory Kristof: 45 up; Annie Griffiths Belt: 15 lo; Sarah Leen: 11 lo, 31 up; Michael Lewis: 16 up; Gerd Ludwig: 43 up; George F. Mobley: 14 up, 33 lo 50 up; Tom Murphy: 23 lo; Paul Nicklen: 17 up, 55 lo; Richard Nowitz: 3 left, 13 lo, 38-39, 46 lo, 53 lo; Richard Olsenius: TP, 2-3, 26-27, 35 up, 35 lo; Chris Rainer: 15 up; Jim Richardson: 23 up, 42 lo; Rick Rickman: 2 left, 6-7; Norbert Rosing: 20 up, 42 up, 47 up; Joel Sartore: 25 up; Tomasz Tomaszewski: 31 lo; Michael Yamashita: 10 up; Burk Uzzle: 53 up.

Text copyright © 2007 National Geographic Society
Hardcover ISBN: 978-1-4263-0025-7
First paperback printing 2009
Paperback ISBN: 978-1-4263-0573-3
Published by the National Geographic Society.
All rights reserved. Reproduction of the whole or any part of the contents without written permission from the National Geographic Society is strictly prohibited. For information about special discounts for bulk purchases, contact National Geographic Special Sales: ngspecsales@ngs.org

For more information, please call 1-800-NGS-LINE (647-5463) or write to the following address:

NATIONAL GEOGRAPHIC SOCIETY
1145 17th Street N.W.
Washington, D.C. 20036-4688 U.S.A.

Visit the Society's Web site at www.nationalgeographic.com

Printed in the United States of America

Series design by Jim Hiscott.
The body text is set in Avenir; Knockout.
The display text is set in Matrix Script.

Front Cover—Top: Cowboy rides a bull at the Calgary Stampede; Low far left: Combines harvest wheat on a farm in Saskatchewan that sits astride the Trans-Canada Highway; Low left: Canadian mounted policeman saluting; Low right: Twilight view of the city of Vancouver, British Columbia; Low far right: A mother polar bear and her cub.

Page 1—Inuits cross Ferguson Lake, Nunavut; Icon image on spine, Contents page, and throughout: Maple leaves in fall

09/WOR/1

Produced through the worldwide resources of the National Geographic Society

John M. Fahey, Jr., *President and Chief Executive Officer*; Gilbert M. Grosvenor, *Chairman of the Board*; Nina D. Hoffman, *Executive Vice President, President of Book Publishing Group*

National Geographic Staff for this Book

Nancy Laties Feresten, *Vice President, Editor-in-Chief of Children's Books*
Bea Jackson, *Director of Design and Illustration*
Virginia Koeth, *Project Editor*
Lori Epstein, *Illustrations Editor*
Stacy Gold, Nadia Hughes, *Illustrations Research Editors*
Carl Mehler, *Director of Maps*
Priyanka Lamichhane, *Assistant Editor*
R. Gary Colbert, *Production Director*
Lewis R. Bassford, *Production Manager*
Maryclare Tracy, Nicole Elliott, *Manufacturing Managers*

Brown Reference Group plc. Staff for this Book

Volume Editor: Tom Jackson
Designer: Dave Allen
Picture Manager: Becky Cox
Maps: Martin Darlinson
Artwork: Darren Awuah
Index: Kay Ollerenshaw
Senior Managing Editor: Tim Cooke
Design Manager: Sarah Williams
Children's Publisher: Anne O'Daly
Editorial Director: Lindsey Lowe

About the Author

BRIAN WILLIAMS has written more than 60 books for children, both on his own and with his wife Brenda. He writes about a range of subjects, but especially about history and geography. This is his first book for NATIONAL GEOGRAPHIC.

About the Consultants

DR. TOM CARTER holds the Canada Research Chair in Urban Change and Adaptation at the University of Winnipeg. Educated in Manitoba, Saskatchewan, and Alberta, he is particularly interested in the development of Canada's urban areas and in government policies affecting First Nations peoples.

DR. BEN CECIL is head of the Department of Geography at the University of Regina in Saskatchewan. He was born in Ontario and has lived throughout Canada. He is particularly interested in the relationship between Canada's geography and business and in the development of Canada's cities.